LIGHTNING BOLT BOOKS™

Chinese Giant Salamanders

Nature's Biggest Amphibian

Walt Brody

Lerner Publications ◆ Minneapolis

Lerner Publications Company
An imprint of Lerner Publishing Group, Inc.
241 First Avenue North
Minneapolis, MN 55401 USA

For reading levels and more information, look up this title at www.lernerbooks.com.

Main body text set in Billy Infant Regular. Typeface provided by SparkType.

Editor: Brianna Kaiser

Library of Congress Cataloging-in-Publication Data

Names: Brody, Walt, 1978- author.
Title: Chinese giant salamanders : nature's biggest amphibian / Walt Brody.
Description: Minneapolis : Lerner Publications, [2024] | Series: Lightning Bolt books - nature's most massive animals | Includes bibliographical references and index. | Audience: Ages 6-9 | Audience: Grades 2-3 | Summary: "Do you know what the largest amphibians are? Giant salamanders! Emerging readers will love learning all kinds of fun facts about these unusual, massive, and fascinating creatures"— Provided by publisher.
Identifiers: LCCN 2023005915 (print) | LCCN 2023005916 (ebook) | ISBN 9798765608418 (library binding) | ISBN 9798765615386 (epub)
Subjects: LCSH: Chinese giant salamander—Juvenile literature. | BISAC: JUVENILE NONFICTION / Animals / Reptiles & Amphibians
Classification: LCC QL668.C24 B76 2024 (print) | LCC QL668.C24 (ebook) | DDC 597.8/5—dc23/eng/20230223

LC record available at https://lccn.loc.gov/2023005915
LC ebook record available at https://lccn.loc.gov/2023005916

Manufactured in the United States of America
1-1009286-51495-4/21/2023

Table of Contents

Meet the Chinese Giant Salamander

A fish swims up a river in China. Suddenly, something sucks the fish into its mouth. It's a Chinese giant salamander!

Chinese giant salamanders have smooth, wet skin.

Chinese giant salamanders are the biggest amphibians on Earth. They can grow to 6.5 feet (2 m) long and weigh up to 110 pounds (50 kg).

Egg to Adult

Chinese giant salamanders live their whole lives underwater. They begin life as eggs. The eggs soak in water and grow.

Chinese giant salamander eggs

The eggs hatch between one and two months after they are laid. They hatch quicker when the water is warmer. The hatched larvae are about 1.2 inches (3 cm) long.

The larvae have gills. They use these to breathe. The gills will fall off after the larvae grow to 8 to 10 inches (20 to 25 cm) in length.

A boy looking at a young Chinese giant salamander

A man feeds young Chinese giant salamanders.

Larvae start feeding after thirty days. They become adults in five to six years. Chinese giant salamanders keep growing for their entire lives.

A River Home

Chinese giant salamanders live in China. They are mostly found in China's Yangtze, Yellow, and Pearl rivers.

An adult Chinese giant salamander

Unlike young Chinese giant salamanders, adults do not have gills. **They absorb oxygen through their skin.**

Chinese giant salamanders are dark brown with black and red spots.

Their skin color and spots help them blend into the riverbed. This helps protect them from predators.

Chinese giant salamanders are also predators. They eat fish, frogs, worms, insects, and crabs. **They hunt by sucking their prey into their mouths.**

Chinese giant salamanders even eat other salamanders.

Long Lives

Chinese giant salamanders breed in the summer months when the water is warmer. The young can grow faster in the warm water.

A male Chinese giant salamander

Chinese giant salamanders

The eggs hatch and the larvae will be on their own. The young can breed when they are mature in five or six years.

Male Chinese giant salamanders protect the eggs from predators.

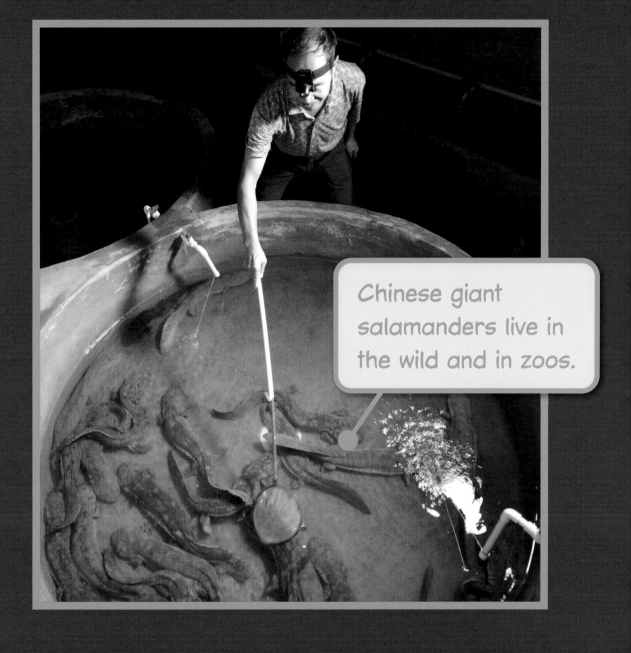

Chinese giant salamanders live in the wild and in zoos.

Chinese giant salamanders can live to be more than sixty years old. These salamanders have the longest life span of any amphibian.

Chinese giant salamanders are endangered. Humans hunt these salamanders. Water pollution and climate change make the water they live in unsafe.

A fisher in China

18

A Chinese giant salamander in a zoo

With less hunting and pollution, these huge animals can grow up and raise more Chinese giant salamanders.

Chinese Giant Salamander Diagram

Head

Tail

Eye

Mouth

Foot

Fun
Facts

- There are three types of giant salamanders: Chinese giant salamanders, Japanese giant salamanders, and North American giant salamanders.

- Albinism is a condition that affects an animal's coloring. Salamanders with albinism are white or orange instead of brown.

- Giant salamanders can bark, whine, and hiss. They sometimes make sounds like a crying human baby!

Glossary

amphibian: a type of animal that lives in the water that includes frogs, salamanders, and toads

breed: to mate to produce babies

endangered: a type of animal that is in danger of becoming extinct

fertilize: to make able to produce babies

gill: an organ used to breathe in oxygen from water

larva: an early stage of a Chinese giant salamander's life

pollution: when harmful materials contaminate the environment

predator: an animal that gets food mostly by killing and eating other animals

prey: an animal that is hunted or killed by another animal for food

Learn More

Britannica Kids: Salamander
https://kids.britannica.com/kids/article/salamander/390150

Golusky, Jackie. *Komodo Dragons: Nature's Biggest Lizard*. Minneapolis: Lerner Publications, 2024.

Hughes, Catherine D. *Little Kids First Big Book of Reptiles and Amphibians*. Washington, DC: National Geographic Partners, 2020.

Humphrey, Natalie. *Chinese Giant Salamander: Huge Amphibian.* Buffalo: PowerKids Press, 2024.

Kidadl: Fun Giant Salamander Facts For Kids
https://kidadl.com/facts/animals/giant-salamander-facts

Kiddle: Amphibian Facts for Kids
https://kids.kiddle.co/Amphibian

Index

Photo Acknowledgments

Images used: Ian Winslow/Shutterstock, p. 4; AP Photo/Imaginechina, p. 5; Danny Ye/Alamy, p. 6; Xinhua/Alamy, pp. 7, 9, 17; GOH CHAI HIN/AFP/Getty Images, p .8; Pawika Tongtavee/Shutterstock, p. 10; Best View Stock/Getty Images, p. 11; Nature Picture Library/Alamy, p. 12; tristan tan/Shutterstock, pp. 13, 14; Animal vision/Alamy, pp. 15, 16; Tutti Frutti/Shutterstock, p. 18; Billy Hustace/Getty Images, p. 19; Natural Visions/Alamy, p. 20.

Cover: Best View Stock/Alamy.